Tuscany
IN THE KITCHEN

30 recipes that are too good to miss!

MARIA TERESA DI MARCO - MARIE CÉCILE FERRÉ
PHOTOGRAPHY BY MAURIZIO MAURIZI

PICCOLI SPUNTINI

Guido Tommasi Editore
dal 1999

Summary

"It would be difficult to find cleaner fields anywhere; one cannot see the smallest clod of earth; the soil is as clean as if it had been sifted. Wheat seems to find here all the conditions most favourable to its growth, and does very well".
Goethe, *Italian Journey,* 1786 *(translation by W. H. Auden and Elizabeth Mayer)*

On second thoughts Tuscan cuisine is in danger of becoming an illusion, perhaps because it basically resembles the blunt and instantly recognizable way Tuscan people speak, a dialect so flawless it can scarcely be called a dialect. It is a cuisine based on produce from the land and on bread, seasoned with salt and spices, cooked for hours, a plain-spoken cuisine which makes itself heard. Ribbed tomatoes ennoble bread soup, Certaldo onions exalt onion soup, unsalted Tuscan bread covets the first extra virgin olive oil off the press, salami with fennel seeds and red wine and peppery Tuscan beef stew, while tripe craves its broth and Siena spaghetti (pici) its garlic sauce.

More than in any other part of Italy here it is simplicity which counts, although, on closer look, it is actually not so simple after all. Forget the "Tuscany" trademark which pretends to elevate it yet which really fails to acknowledge it being unfamiliar with it. Because if Tuscan soup is bread soup, ribollita makes it into something different, which needs to be preserved for posterity without necessarily locking up the soup or, indeed, the whole of Tuscan cuisine in a museum display cabinet. Food and the love of food seems to us, in Tuscany more than anywhere else, a living thing. You make it with the ingredients you have to hand yet you really make it. So we have removed lids, peeked into Mario's kitchen cupboards and Marcella's saucepans, picked mushrooms with Matteo in the Trebbia woods and been intoxicated by landscapes and flavours. The recipes you will find in this book are just some of the Tuscan recipes we love, a mere taste of that variegated Tuscan gastronomic panorama, a brief segment of a long journey, at the end of which it is we who have changed, while Tuscan cuisine remains the same, intertwined with its history and its land.

à Léo qui aurait aimé

ANNA'S SPLEEN CROUTONS

For 6 people

- 300 g of spleen
- 200 g of minced beef
- 4-5 chicken livers
- 600 ml of vegetable broth
- half a glass of white wine
- half a glass of sweet white Italian dessert wine
- half a tube of anchovy paste or 4-5 anchovies
- 40 g of ground capers
- 1 onion
- extra virgin olive oil
- salt

Sauté the onion in two tablespoons of extra virgin olive oil and a little water. When the onion is transparent add the minced meat and cook for a few minutes.
Parboil the livers, which you have previously cleaned of any traces of bile, for ten minutes. Carefully clean the spleen, removing all the skin. If you have never done this before ask your butcher to do it for you.
Once the livers are cooked, rinse them thoroughly, add them to the minced meat and the spleen and blend in the mixer.
Transfer the mixture into a small saucepan heating on the stove and brown it. Then add the white wine and the sweet white dessert wine. When the wine has evaporated cover with vegetable broth. Cook over a low heat for at least two hours. Then add the anchovy paste, check the salt and finish with the ground capers.
Turn the heat off, leave to cool and serve with Tuscan bread.

CECINA (Chickpea Bread)

Cecina is a close relative of Ligurian chickpea flour bread and it is no coincidence that it is a typical dish of Lunigiana although it is also found all long the Northern coast of Tuscany, in Versilia and in Livorno.

For 4 people

- 200 g of chickpea flour
- 750 ml of cold water
- 4 tablespoons of extra virgin olive oil
- a teaspoon of salt

Blend the chickpea flour with the water a little at a time taking care not to form lumps. Leave it to rest for a few hours, then eliminate the froth which will have formed on the surface with a perforated spoon. Add 3 tablespoons of extra virgin olive oil and the salt.

Pour the mixture into a round low-sided baking tray, calculating that the cecina must be no more than one centimetre high. Place in a piping hot oven for about 30-40 minutes. When it is time to serve it you can add ground black pepper if you like.

BREAD SOUP

For 6 people

- 1 kg of cannellini (white kidney) beans (or pinto beans)
- 1 bunch of purple kale
- ¼ of Savoy cabbage
- 1 onion
- 2 carrots
- 2 potatoes
- 2 sticks of celery
- 1 400 g tin of tomatoes
- 300 g of stale Tuscan bread
- 5 tablespoons of extra virgin olive oil
- salt and pepper

Cook the beans for approximately half an hour after being sure to soak them overnight. Sauté the onion in the oil and then add all the previously washed and cubed vegetables. Cook them in the water you cooked the beans in. After approximately quarter of an hour add the tinned tomatoes and simmer for about ten minutes. Then add the beans, half of them creamed in a food mill and half of them whole, and continue to cook over a gentle heat for about 2-3 hours. During this phase of preparation it is important to be extra careful the soup doesn't stick to the pan.

Slice the bread thinly and keep placing layers of bread, vegetables and broth, until you have used up all the ingredients, in the bowls you plan to serve the soup in. Add salt and pepper and serve.

RIBOLLITA (Tuscan Bread Soup)

Since 2001 there has been a certified recipe for genuine Ribollita Doc, registered by the Florentine Delegation of the Accademia Italiana with a solicitor. We can only delight in the existence of this official version, which has the noble task of defending a dish, which is the very essence of Tuscany, from the many mangled versions fobbed off on oblivious tourists even outside Tuscany. However, it must be said that, as with every everyday regional dish, there are many versions of *ribollita* and all are authentic to some extent. So, Up with *Ribollita*! But remember it is a dish that is still cooked in Tuscan homes as well as a notary deed.

Ribollita is none other than bread soup made with leftover day-old bread, having made sure to boil the bread with all the other ingredients. This is how it gets its name.

Cook it, or rather cook it again, until it comes to the boil and, before serving, drizzle some extra virgin olive oil on top of each bowl.

CHICKPEA SOUP

For 4 people

- 350 g of dried chickpeas (pink chickpeas from Reggello are the best)
- 1 tablespoon of tomato paste
- 4 tablespoons of extra virgin olive oil
- 2 sprigs of rosemary
- 2 cloves of garlic
- 2 bay leaves
- salt

The evening before rinse the chickpeas in cold water and leave them to soak with a tablespoon of salt. The following morning drain them, put them in a heavy-bottomed pot, cover them with plenty of water (four fingers above the level of the chickpeas), add the bay leaves and cook over a low heat for at least two hours, adding the salt only towards the end.
Drain the chickpeas and purée them in a food mill, put the mixture back in the pot, add the tomato paste and cook over a very low heat.
Brown the sliced garlic and the rosemary in a separate pot. Once the oil has absorbed the flavours, remove the garlic and rosemary and add the oil to the creamed chickpea mixture. Cook for approximately ten minutes more and then serve.

MUSHROOM AND BEAN SOUP

For 4 people

- 400 g of mushrooms (cèpes and other varieties)
- 400 g of pinto beans
- 2 cloves of garlic
- 1 sprig of field balm
- 4 tablespoons of extra virgin olive oil
- salt and pepper
- 4 slices of Tuscan bread

Leave the beans to soak overnight and then boil them in plenty of salted water. Purée half of them in a food mill and leave the others whole in approximately 1 litre of the water they were cooked in. Blend the puréed beans and the whole beans in their broth.
Clean the mushrooms, give them a quick rinse under cold running water and chop them into medium-sized chunks. Fry the chunks with the garlic and the field balm in the hot oil. Add the bean broth to the mushrooms and cook them for a few minutes, adding salt and pepper. Make sure the soup is nice and sloppy so you can serve it with some slices of toasted bread.

ACQUA COTTA (Clear Soup)

For 4 people

- 2 red Tuscan onions
- 2 carrots
- 1 stick of leafy celery
- 300 g of tinned tomatoes
- 250 g of chards (or other leafy green vegetables but not spinach)
- 4 eggs
- 4 slices of 3-4 day-old Tuscan bread
- 1 clove of garlic
- 5 tablespoons of extra virgin olive oil
- grated Pecorino cheese to taste
- salt and pepper

Slice the onions and lightly fry them in oil in a large frying pan with high sides. As soon as they are transparent and thoroughly stewed, add the coarsely chopped chard and the carrot and celery chopped into chunks. Cook for a few minutes until the vegetables absorb all the flavours, then add the crushed tinned tomatoes and cover with about one and a half litres of water. Add salt and pepper and cook for thirty to forty minutes.

Five minutes before serving toast the slices of bread and rub them with the garlic, then put one in each bowl. Carefully break the eggs straight into the frying pan, cook for another five minutes as you would a poached egg and then serve each dinner guest with two ladlefuls of soup and an egg. Sprinkle with grated Pecorino cheese and a little more pepper.

Acqua cotta is a typical soup from Maremma which, just like *ribollita*, has many variants depending on customs, tastes and, above all, availability of ingredients. Indeed, once an extremely impoverished land, Maremma invented a soup whose principal ingredient is water; all the rest is added richness.

CARABACCIA (Tuscan Onion Soup)

For 4 people

- 4 Tuscan red onions, ideally from Certaldo
- 100 g of peeled and finely ground almonds
- 1 litre of vegetable broth
- 4 tablespoons of extra virgin olive oil
- 1 tablespoon of sugar
- 1 tablespoon of powdered cinnamon
- 1 tablespoon of white wine vinegar
- salt

Finely slice the onions, then stew them for about ten minutes with the oil in a large frying pan until they are soft. Add the almonds mixed with a tablespoon of white wine vinegar and cover with broth. Cook for another thirty minutes.

Add the salt and serve in consommé cups with a sprinkle of powdered cinnamon mixed with the sugar.

This soup has extremely ancient origins and is considered to some extent to be the mother of the celebrated French "soupe aux oignons". Indeed, in France it was Catherine de'Medici who, along with many other refinements, introduced the novel idea of growing onions and tarragon and using both in cooking.

"The soup is ready to eat
And all of us sing as one
We want tomato and bread soup
No sooner said than done!"
Rita Pavone

TOMATO AND BREAD SOUP

For 4 people

- 250 g of stale Tuscan bread
- 4-5 fresh tomatoes (ideally ribbed)
- salt, pepper
- 2 cloves of garlic
- 4 leaves of basil
- 4 tablespoons of extra virgin olive oil + more for the dressing
- 500 ml of vegetable broth

Brown the garlic and basil in the oil. After a few minutes add the tomatoes, previously parboiled and peeled, and bring them to the boil. Then add the broth and the bread cut into very small chunks. Cook the bread soup for a few minutes more, then leave it to rest for about half an hour. Add salt, pepper and fresh basil and dress with a few drops of olive oil. You can eat it cold or hot.
Up with bread soup!

Panzanella is a type of fresh salad made with bread and vegetables dressed with vinegar and oil. One might think of it as the ancestor of pasta or rice salads or even Middle Eastern tabboulé. Actually it has extremely ancient origins. It was even mentioned by Bronzino (an artist rather than a poet) who, since the tomato hadn't yet been introduced (America had already been discovered but the tomato wasn't used in cooking yet), put onions, cucumbers and purslane in it, as well as basil and rocket.

Today there are numerous versions and tomato is used in almost all of them. On the other hand, the orthodoxy of other ingredients is a matter of debate.

LA PANZANELLA DEL BRONZINO (Bronzino's Tuscan Salad)

For 4 people

- 400 g of 3-4 day-old Tuscan bread baked in a wood-fired oven
- 2 Tuscan red onions
- 2 cucumbers
- one cup of purslane
- one bunch of basil
- one bunch of wild rocket
- 3 tablespoons of red wine vinegar
- 5 tablespoons of extra virgin olive oil
- salt

Fill a large bowl with cold water and soak the thickly-sliced bread in it for about ten minutes. Then take the bread out, a handful at a time, squeezing it tightly to drain all the water, and then put it in a large salad bowl.
Slice the onion thinly and peel the cucumbers and slice them too. Rinse the purslane, rocket and basil and chop them coarsely.
Add the vegetables to the squeezed bread, season with salt, vinegar and oil and, finally, add the leaves of basil, rocket and basil. Mix well and leave to rest before serving.

Bronzino's poem:

*"If you want to fly above the stars
then dip some bread and eat until your buttons burst.
A salad made of chopped onion,
purslane and cucumbers
beats any other pleasure in this life.
Just imagine if you were to add
basil and rocket!"*

PICI is a fat spaghetti made of flour and water. It is from Siena but found everywhere in Tuscany. Once it was handmade by rolling the strands of pasta between the palms or by using a pasta-cutter to cut out the pasta shapes. Now it is still very popular but mostly bought from traditional pasta shops and, when it is homemade, it is made with the help of a pasta machine.

PICI IN SPICY GARLIC SAUCE

For 4 people

- 350 g of pici
- 4 large cloves of garlic
- 2 ripe tomatoes
- 1 chilli pepper
- 4 tablespoons of extra virgin olive oil
- plenty of grated Pecorino cheese
- salt and pepper

Cook the pici for 5 minutes in plenty of lightly salted boiling water. In the meantime, pan-fry the peeled and crushed garlic cloves in the extra virgin olive oil with the chilli pepper and then add the deseeded, skinned tomatoes, which have been mashed with a fork, and let them form a pulp. When cooked drain the pici and fold it into the sauce. Add plenty of grated Pecorino cheese and some ground black pepper.

Garlic-lovers can follow the name of the recipe to the letter and leave out the tomato entirely. The pici prove to be extremely flavoursome anyway thanks to the Pecorino cheese and black pepper.

PAPPARDELLE WITH DUCK

This recipe was generously gifted to us by Romeo of Trattoria Mario in Florence. We spent a wonderful morning learning how to make the sauce step by step, from chopping the duck to the final "adjustment" of the herbs and spices. We had worshipped Mario from afar for almost twenty years but after the hours spent in his kitchen we totally surrendered to his charms.

For 10 people

- 1 kg of pappardelle pasta

For the sauce
- 1 kg of duck with all its bones
- 1 kg of minced lean beef
- 1 kg of mixed vegetables and herbs (onions, carrots, celery, bay leaves, garlic and rosemary)
- 300 g of tomato paste
- 300 ml of extra virgin olive oil
- 1 tablespoon of roasting juices (saved from a previous roast)
- 1 tablespoon of ground Tuscan spices (star anise, cinnamon, cloves, coriander, nutmeg, fennel seeds)
- 2 tablespoons of powdered chilli pepper
- 2 ladles of broth
- salt and pepper

Strip the duck by separating the meat from the bones, which should be kept to one side.
Heat the rosemary and the garlic still in its skin (but "castrated", as Romeo puts it, or in other words making a small cut so that it doesn't explode when it is cooked) in some of the oil and sauté the bones over a lively heat. Add salt and pepper and continue to cook.
In a second larger pan sauté the rest of the vegetables and herbs in the remaining oil. When you cannot tell the various vegetables apart add a tablespoon of roasting juices and then add the bones (without the rosemary and garlic) and the broth, which Romeo suggests heating in the same pan you sautéed the bones in. Cook for about ten minutes and then add the minced duck meat. Allow it to absorb the flavours and then add the minced beef. Cook for about 30 minutes and then "fix" it (as Romeo puts it, meaning adding salt), add the chilli pepper and the Tuscan spices and, finally, the tomato paste and a ladle of warm water. Continue to cook covered over a low heat for about 2 hours.

GIUSEPPINA'S BOILED TRIPE

For 4/5 people

- 1.5 kg of tripe
- 1 carrot
- 1 onion
- 2 sticks of celery
- 2-3 tomatoes
- salt
- green sauce, as a side dish (see below)

Rinse the tripe, put it in a high-sided pan together with the vegetables and cover with cold water (at least two fingers). Add the salt and let it boil over a low heat for about 3 hours if the tripe is raw. If the tripe is cooked then an hour is sufficient.

Chop the tripe and serve it with a side dish of a light, sweet sauce made of parsley, celery (including the leaves), a little garlic, extra virgin olive oil, salt and pepper.

Giuseppina ran a grocery store with her son in San Niccolò in Florence. It was one of those delicatessens which are the hub of a neighbourhood partly because you can buy ready-cooked delicacies there. However, in time and with the opening of a supermarket in the area, the shop needed to be revamped and so it was turned into something quite unique, with a large counter in the middle and a clear mission: soup and boiled meats.

PEPPERY BEEF STEW

For 4 people

- 800 g of beef stewing steak
- 4 cloves of garlic
- a handful of black peppercorns (about 10 g)
- a bottle of classic Chianti (about 750 ml)
- salt
- sage
- rosemary

Chop the meat into not too small pieces and put it in a heavy-bottomed pan (an earthenware pot is ideal). Add the garlic, the peppercorns, the sage and the rosemary and cover everything with the wine. Cook over a lowish heat for about 2 and a half hours. When it is almost cooked add the salt and a little more ground pepper to taste.
This peppery dish is served, like a lot of other Tuscan food, with a side dish of toasted bread.

In the original recipe, from the bread ovens of Impruneta, beef fat, which gradually melts and impregnates the meat, should be slathered on the bottom of the pan. But this is a dish for rugged men used to heavy labour and a huge expenditure of energy.

SWEET AND SOUR RABBIT

For 6 people

- 1 approximately 1.5 kg rabbit
- 1 onion
- 2 small carrots
- 1 stick of celery
- 6 tablespoons of extra virgin olive oil
- 1 tablespoon of flour
- broth

For the dolce forte:

- 30 g of dark chocolate shavings
- 40 g of raisins
- 30 g of pine nuts
- 30 g of candied citron
- 1 tablespoon of sugar
- 2 tablespoons of red wine vinegar

Gut and clean the rabbit and keep it to one side. Finely chop the vegetables and brown them in the extra virgin olive oil. As soon as they begin to sizzle add the rabbit chopped into pieces and sauté until golden on all sides. Add a tablespoon of flour to the cooking juices and then add broth or hot water and cook for another 30-40 minutes.

In the meantime, prepare the dolce forte by mixing all the ingredients in a large bowl. When the rabbit is almost cooked, pour it into the pan and stir well with a wooden spoon. Cook for another 10-15 minutes, then let the dish rest for a few hours or a whole day, so that all the ingredients are thoroughly blended. Heat and serve.

The original and more traditional recipe required hare instead of rabbit but, partly because hare is hard to find, we chose rabbit. Other meats, above all wild boar, can be cooked in dolce forte, while there are also dolce forte recipes for dried salted codfish and sardines.

FLORENTINE TRIPE

For 5 people

- 1 kg cleaned tripe
- 1 approximately 100 g onion
- 200-300 g of tomato paste
- 50 ml of extra virgin olive oil
- 20 g of butter

Sizzle some thinly sliced onion in the oil over a lively (Remo says "violent") heat without worrying about it sticking. When you have almost reached the point of no return add the tomato paste and stir energetically as the tomato tends to form a patina on the bottom of the pan and burn. As soon as the tomato has begun to bind add the cold tripe and stir for a few minutes until the tripe begins to sweat. Cover the pan, lower the heat and continue to cook, stirring occasionally. Tripe, says Remo, must always simmer and never "gallop".

Calculate an hour or an hour and a half for cooking, then turn off the heat and add a small pat of butter, leave it to rest and, if you like, serve it with grated Parmesan cheese, although Remo wouldn't approve.

This is another recipe for which we are indebted to Remo, who invited us to spend the morning at "Mario's" so we could observe each of the phases of preparation. By ten o'clock after listening to his advice and explanations and stories and after he had lifted the lid off several times so we could have a good sniff we were as ravenous as wolves.

TUSCAN MIXED FRY

For 6 people

- 800 g of lamb cutlets
- 800 g of rabbit
- 800 of chicken
- 3 courgettes
- 4 small artichokes
- 8 pumpkin flowers
- 5-6 eggs
- flour
- breadcrumbs
- salt and pepper
- oil for frying

First prepare the vegetables. Chop the artichokes into wedges and remove the thistles and chop the courgettes into strips. Leave the pumpkin flowers whole but remove their pistils.
Beat the lamb cutlets and coat them first with the egg and then with the breadcrumbs.
Roll the chicken and rabbit pieces first in the egg and then in the flour. Dust the artichokes with flour and dip the courgettes and pumpkin flowers in a batter made of water and flour.
Fry in plenty of piping hot oil: first the lamb, then the chicken and rabbit and finally the vegetables. Little by little, as each ingredient is cooked, lay them out on sheets of kitchen towel, sprinkle with salt and keep warm, for instance in the oven, which you have turned off and which is now cooling down.

In Tuscany a mixed fry is a party and people tend to fry absolutely anything. Here too you can add whatever you like to the meat and vegetables: veal, sweetbreads or brain, cauliflower, gobbi (cardoons), sage or even bread.

MARCELLA'S WILD BOAR STEW

For 4 people

- 800 g of wild boar
- 2 onions
- 4 sprigs of rosemary
- 8 leaves of sage
- 3 cloves of garlic
- 1 glass of white wine
- 2 400 g tins of tomatoes
- parsley
- salt and pepper

Soak the wild boar overnight in cold water with half of the rosemary, the sage and a whole onion. The morning after scald the wild boar in water for about a quarter of an hour so as to get rid of the gamey smell, then drain and rinse the meat thoroughly under hot running water.

Sauté the garlic, an onion, the sage, the rest of the rosemary and a little parsley and brown the meat in it. After about twenty minutes add the white wine and let it evaporate over a low heat for about a quarter of an hour. Then add the tinned tomatoes and cook for at least two and a half hours over a low heat. Add salt and pepper.

Marcella's tip for toning down the excessively strong taste of wild boar is to add a walnut in its shell while it is cooking.

STEAK AND ENTRECOTE

With regard to steak, or what people who are not from Florence call Florentine steak, it is perhaps more useful to provide a guide to what you absolutely mustn't do rather than a recipe that tells you what you should do.

First of all, there is the source of the meat: Florentine steak must come from Chianina steer no more than two years of age. The meat must be hung in a refrigerating room for 15-20 days.

Secondly, there is the cut: it must be T shaped, or rather cut from the loin (from near the lumbar vertebra near the tail), with the (T-shaped) bone in the middle dividing the tenderloin and the sirloin. If there is no bone it is an entrecote, which may be delicious but is not Florentine steak.

As for weight and height it should weigh no more than one and a half kilos and be about 4-5 centimetres thick.

With regard to cooking there are some strict bans: never marinate in oil, never add salt before it is done, never prick with a fork or, worse still, with a knife. It is ideally cooked on charcoal (of holm oak, oak or olive). Griddles made of any material are out of the question. Just use a grill placed about ten centimetres above the embers.

It may only be eaten rare: a little charred on the outside but soft and pink on the inside. This requires 5 minutes of searing on each side.

For the dressing: salt is allowed, indeed compulsory (but must only be added when the meat is cooked), and pepper may be used in moderation. No oil or lemon.

It sounds tricky, and perhaps it is, but it is well worth the effort.

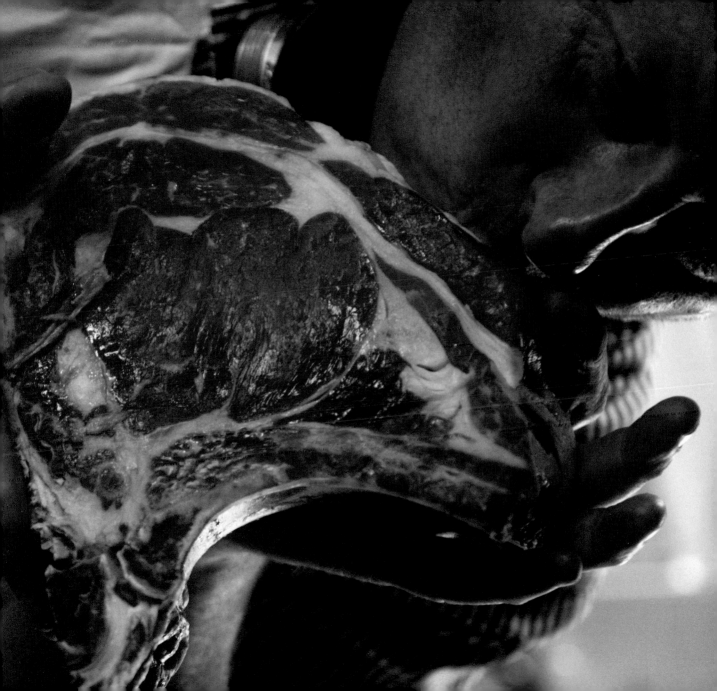

CACCIUCCO ALLA LIVORNESE (Livornese Fish Stew)

For 6 people

- 800 g of fish for broth (scorpionfish, grey gurnard, viper weever, conger eel, dory, etc.)
- 800 g of octopus and cuttlefish
- 800 g of dogfish
- 6 Mediterranean slipper lobsters

- 400 g of tinned tomatoes
- 1 large onion
- 1 carrot
- 1 stick of celery
- one small bunch of parsley
- 2 cloves of garlic
- ½ a chilli pepper
- 1 glass of red wine
- 6 slices of Tuscan bread
- 6 tablespoons of extra virgin olive oil
- broth
- salt and pepper

Clean the fish: remove the fins and the guts, but not the heads.
Clean the squid and the octopus and chop into large pieces.
Remove the skin from the dogfish and cut it into slices.
Finely chop the onion, carrot, celery, chilli pepper and parsley and brown everything in the extra virgin olive oil. As soon as the onion is golden, add the shellfish and cover with the wine. Increase the heat, allow the wine to evaporate, then add the tinned tomatoes and lower the heat, add the other fish and cover with a few ladles of broth or hot water. Cook over a low heat for about 40 minutes, add salt and pepper and serve the soup with slices of toasted bread rubbed with garlic.

RED MULLET LIVORNO STYLE

For 4 people

- 1 kg of medium sized red mullet (weighing about 100 g each)
- 300 g of tinned tomatoes
- 2 cloves of garlic
- 6 tablespoons of extra virgin olive oil
- 1 small bunch of parsley
- salt and pepper

Clean the red mullet, scale them and remove the fins, then wash them thoroughly inside and out.
Mince the garlic with the parsley and sauté the mixture in the oil in a rather large pan. As soon as the garlic begins to blanch add the tinned tomatoes and mash with a wooden spoon.
Cook the sauce for a few minutes, add salt and pepper and arrange the red mullet in the pan bearing in mind you will not be able to move them. Indeed, red mullet cook quickly and are extremely delicate.
Cook for about ten minutes moistening the red mullet with their own juices and shaking the pan from time to time. When you are about to serve the dish add salt and a little more chopped parsley.

SQUID WITH CHARD

For 6 people

- 1 kg of cuttlefish or small squid
- 1 kg of raw chard (or spinach)
- 250 g of tomato purée
- 1 large golden onion
- 1 carrot
- 1 stick of celery
- 1 glass of white wine
- 2 cloves of garlic
- 6 tablespoons of extra virgin olive oil
- salt and pepper

Remove the leaves from the chards and leave some of the soft part of the stalk. Wash the chards thoroughly and then boil them briefly in lightly salted water. Drain them, leave them to cool and then wring them out with your hands forming a ball which you will keep to one side.
Clean the cuttlefish (or the squid), wash them under running water and then cut them into narrow ribbons, wash them again and then pat them with a dry cloth.
Mince the onion, the carrot and the stick of celery and sauté the mixture in a large heavy-bottomed pan together with two cloves of garlic with their skins. As soon as the mixture begins to sizzle and turn golden, add the pieces of cuttlefish, brown them and then add water, salt and pepper. Then pour in the wine, increase the heat and let it evaporate. When you can no longer smell the wine fumes add the tomato purée and stir thoroughly adding, if necessary, a few ladles of hot water. Cook covered for about ten minutes, add the coarsely chopped chards and continue to cook for about another ten minutes, although a great deal depends on how tender the cuttlefish are.

BEANS IN TOMATO SAUCE

For 4 people

- 400 g dried cannellini (white kidney) or toscanelli beans
- 3 cloves of garlic
- 3 tablespoons of extra virgin olive oil
- 5 ripe tomatoes (or 400 g of tinned tomatoes)
- 5-6 leaves of sage
- salt and pepper

Soak the beans overnight in a bowl of water. The day after cook them in plenty of water and salt for about twenty minutes.
Sauté the garlic and sage in the oil. As soon as the garlic becomes transparent add the beans and after a few minutes add the tomatoes. Continue to cook until the beans are soft. Add salt and pepper and serve.

FLORENTINE PEAS

For 4 people

- 1 kg of fresh green peas
- 50 g of cooked ham or bacon
- 1 tablespoon of sugar
- 1 fresh bulb of garlic
- 2 tablespoons of extra virgin olive oil
- a bunch of parsley
- salt and pepper

Shell the peas and put them in a pot with the extra virgin olive oil, the fresh garlic cut into rings, the parsley, the sugar and the ham (or the bacon) cut into strips.
Cover with water and cook over a very low heat without a lid. When the peas begin to boil add salt and pepper and continue to cook for 40-45 minutes over a low heat.

VEGETABLE FLAN

For 6/8 people

For the filling:
- 1.5 kg of chards
- 250 g of ricotta
- 2 eggs
- 50 g of grated Pecorino cheese
- 30 g of breadcrumbs
- 1 tablespoon of extra virgin olive oil
- salt and pepper

For the puff pastry:
- 300 g of flour
- 4 tablespoons of extra virgin olive oil
- water

Separate the green leaves from the stalks, wash them, chop them, cover them in salt and leave them in a colander until all the water has drained. Once this is done squeeze them tightly using your hands and mix them with the ricotta. Add the beaten egg, the Pecorino cheese and the breadcrumbs and then season with a little black pepper and a tablespoon of extra virgin olive oil.

Make the puff pastry by kneading the flour with the oil and as much water (about a cup) as you need to obtain a compact but workable dough. Divide the dough into two parts and roll out into two thin sheets of pastry. They should be the thickness of tagliatelle.

Stretch the larger sheet to fit the bottom of a testo (the special terracotta pot typical of Lunigiana) lined with greaseproof paper and fill it with the vegetable mixture. Cover with the second sheet of pastry and make a rim to seal the pie. Brush the top of the pie with a little extra virgin olive oil blended with a drop of water and pierce it with a fork to let the steam out. Cover with a lid and bake in a preheated oven at 200°C for about an hour.

As well as cèpes and sage people fry anything and everything in Tuscany: borace leaves when they are in season, artichokes, gobbi (cardoons), pumpkin flowers and even acacia flowers. Moreover, there is a proverb that says "even a slipper tastes good fried", and it's probably true!

FRIED SAGE

For 4 people

- 30 nice big sage leaves
- anchovy paste to taste
- 1 egg
- 50 g of flour
- extra virgin olive oil
- salt

Wash the sage leaves thoroughly, dry them on a cloth, then pair off the leaves filling them with a little anchovy paste.
Make the batter with the egg and flour. Dip the leaves in the batter and fry them in plenty of piping hot extra virgin olive oil.
Sprinkle with salt and eat warm.

ANNA'S GRAPE BREAD

For 6 people

- 350 g of flour
- grapes to taste (but don't stint!)
- 3 tablespoons of sugar
- 3 tablespoons of olive oil
- 1 block of brewer's yeast

Dissolve the yeast in half a cup of water with the sugar and three tablespoons of flour. Add this mixture to the rest of the flour making a well in the middle, and knead on a flat surface. Form a ball and leave the dough to rise for about two hours.
Once the dough has risen divide it into two parts and roll it out into two sheets of pastry. Use one sheet to line a greased tin, lay the grapes which have been previously washed on top and cover with the second sheet of pastry.
Spread the surface with the rest of the grapes, a little sugar and a little olive oil. Cook in a hot oven at 180°C for about half an hour.

GIAMPIERO'S SPICY BISCUITS

For 12/15 people

- 350 ml of water
- 1 kg of sugar
- 1 orange
- 1 kg of flour
- 1 handful of candied peel
- 15 g of aniseed
- 10 g of cinnamon
- 15 g of baking powder
- 1 handful of walnuts

Put the water, sugar and orange peel, removing the zest and cutting it into small squares, into a pan. Boil for 6 minutes, remove from the flame, add the flour and blend thoroughly. Add the walnuts, a handful of candied peel, the aniseed, the cinnamon and the baking powder.
Dust the pastry board with flour, place the dough on it and knead until firm, adding a little flour at a time. Form a block and keep to one side. Taking small amounts of dough, make little sausage shapes and cut them into discs measuring about 3 centimetres in diameter. Press down gently in the centre (to make a small dip), and arrange the cavallucci in a pan greased with butter and dusted with flour. Bake in the oven at 180°C for 15 minutes.

PANFORTE

For 6/8 people

- 200 g of mixed candied peel
- 25 g of candied orange peel
- 175 g of sugar
- 175 g of almonds with their peel
- 75 g of flour
- 1 tablespoon of cinnamon
- 1 tablespoon of black pepper
- ½ tablespoon of mace
- ½ tablespoon of round cloves
- ½ tablespoon of powdered coriander
- icing sugar

Finely chop the candied peel, add the spices and sift the flour over top of the mixture, mixing it in little by little. Keep to one side. Make a syrup by heating the sugar with a little water over a low heat. As soon as it coats the spoon remove it from the heat. Add the syrup to the mixture of flour, candied peel and spices and then add the almonds with their peel. Stir carefully and energetically until it is all smoothly blended.

Cut a disc measuring about 19 cm in diameter from a sheet of wafer paper and line a spring-form cake tin or a disposable aluminium tin with it. Spread the mixture on top and level it with the back of a spoon.
Bake in the oven for 20-25 minutes at 180°C.
Leave the *panforte* to cool, turn it out of the tin and sprinkle it with icing sugar.

MARCELLA'S CUSTARD PIE

For 6 people

- 100 g of butter
- 1 egg
- 1 yolk
- 250 g of flour
- 100 g of sugar
- ½ sachet of yeast
- 40 g of pine nuts

For the custard:

- 4 yolks
- 500 ml of milk
- 50 g of flour
- 100 g of sugar

For the custard:

Bring the milk to the boil and leave it to cool. Mix the yolks with the sugar and flour. When the milk is warm add it to the mixture and put everything back over the heat. Keep stirring and wait until the custard is sufficiently thick.

For the dough:

Combine the butter at room temperature with the sugar and then add the egg, the flour and the powdered yeast. Divide the pastry into two portions. Roll out one portion and use it to line a round tin measuring about 30 cm in diameter that has been greased and dusted with flour. Cover with the custard and the second portion of rolled out pastry.
Sprinkle the pine nuts on top and brush with egg yolk. Cook in a preheated oven at 180°C for about 45 minutes.

It's delicious, trust us on this!

PANDIRAMERINO (Currant Buns)

For 8 people

- 800 g of bread dough
- 200 g of raisins
- 8 tablespoons of extra virgin olive oil
- 5 tablespoons of sugar
- 1 sprig of rosemary

Strip the needles from the sprig of rosemary and chop them coarsely. On a pastry board dusted with flour knead the bread dough and roll it out thinly. Place the sugar, the raisins and the rosemary in the centre and combine all the ingredients by folding the dough over and over several times. Knead energetically adding 5 tablespoons of oil one at a time. When the dough is smooth divide it up into 8 small buns.

Arrange them at a distance from one another on a tin lined with greaseproof paper and make two horizontal and two vertical cuts on each bun so as to form a grid shape. Leave the buns to rise for an hour covered with a cloth, then brush with the remaining oil and bake in a preheated oven at 180°C for about 30 minutes.

Sweet and biscuits

Acknowledgments

Our book of Tuscan cuisine owes many people a huge debt of gratitude. We would like say a big thank you to Guido Tommasi, without whom this book would not have been written. It was while we were in conversation with him that the idea began to take shape, an idea which eventually turned into a challenge. His trust in us enabled us to see the project through. A heartfelt thank you goes to Alessandra who was with us from start to finish. Thank you Giusy, who found time to dedicate to the project in the midst of wedding preparations, thank you Laura for your painstaking and discreet hunt for typos and thank you Tommaso for your sensitive work on the colours and typeface.

Thank you to Maria Cristina Diaz of Azienda Agricola San Donatino and Matteo and Manola of Agriturismo Campolungo of San Donato in Poggio (www.sandonatino.com) for welcoming us with open arms in every season during a year of work.

Thank you Signora Paola Busatti of Tessiture Busatti di Anghiari (www.busatti.com) for your kindness and courtesy and your loving protection of a tradition of absolute beauty.
Thank you Signora Larissa and her husband of the Buratti store in Florence, who invited us to pick out (at times it took us hours) the right pattern and the right shade.
Thank you Spazio Sette store in Rome, which kindly lent us anything we needed and a special thank you to Rosanna and Gabriele who showed us round this miraculous place. Thank you Cristiano (Vecli – Cutler's and gift items), who not only lent us plates, glasses and crockery but also discussed every tiny detail with us.
Thank you Gabriele for the Virginia pottery and especially for the collection of fish plates.
Thank you architects of Moon Design for your loan of Licia Martelli pottery.
Thank you wonderful butchers Dario Cecchini, Simone Fracassi, Danilo Parti, Riccardo Stiaccini, who dedicated their time, attention and meat.
Thank you Forno Pierguidi for their schiacciata with the Florentine lily and the Porciatti bakery of Castellina in Chianti for dividing your bread with the butcher.
Thank you Iole Bartalini of the Castellina in Chianti grocery and La perla del Mare fishmonger's of Principina a Mare.
Thank you Duccio of Azienda Agricola Fontani for your little jars of herbs and Zeb for your lampredotto and your brodo.
Thank you Anna Cella for your mediation, thank you Marzia Morganti Tempestini and the delegation of Club del Fornello di Prato for your biscuit recipe.
We are immensely grateful to Romeo, Fabio and the whole "family" of Trattoria Mario (http://trattoria-mario.com/), who have been making us feel at home for the last twenty years.
We are also hugely grateful to Alessandro Frassica di 'Ino, who has made us feel equally at home though we have known him for less time.

Thank you Manu for always being at our side, thank you Alex and Lorenzo for your linguistic research and for dashing around on trains, thank you Titi for your breakfast and the light in your kitchen, thank you Lugiandro for you know what, thank you Charlotte and Nicolas for waiting before you tucked into the rostinciane, thank you Matteo for the mushrooms, wine and beer and thank you Manola for screeching around the bends in Chianti in your car. Thank you Marcella, Rosanna and Anna for revealing to us the tricks of the trade, thank you Aunt Danielle for your Tuscanised pissaladière, thank you Aunt Pacou for your liqueurs, thank you Enrico for your mushroom soup and thank you Diego for your truffle.
Thank you Silvia, Coriolano, Stefano, Umberto and Macò for eating winter recipes in midsummer, thank you Giampiero for your cavallucci and thank you Valérie and Marianne for sending your advice from Paris. Thank you Daniela for taking our pictures.
Thank you again Luca and Giacomo for your patience.
We are grateful too for the music of Têtes de Bois, which kept us company on this and on other journeys and thank you Timi, Betta, Anna, Francesca, Francy, Maria Chiara, Aldo, Laura and everyone else for your encouragement.

© Guido Tommasi Editore - Datanova S.r.l., 2015

Texts: Maria Teresa Di Marco, Marie Cécile Ferré
Photographs: Maurizio Maurizi
Translation: Judith Mundell
Graphics and page layout: Tommaso Bacciocchi

The fabrics photographed on pages 21, 35, 51 and 57 are by Busatti.
The ceramics photographed on page 49 are by Virginia Ceramiche.
The photographs on pages 43 and 44 were taken inside Macelleria Stiaccini in Castellina in Chianti.
The photograph on page 45 was taken inside Macelleria Cecchini in Panzano.
The photographs on pages 29 and 37 were taken inside Trattoria Mario in Florence.
The photograph on page 31 was taken at Zeb_zuppa e bollito in Firenze.

ISBN: 978 88 67531 103

Printed in China